Characteristics of Faith

A closer look at the many
characteristics of faith in the Christian's
life.

Thomas Couch

Published by

The Spotted Feather, an imprint of Colorful Crow Publishing

Ellijay, Georgia

http://www.colorfulcrowpublishing.com

Published in the United States of America

ISBN 978-1-964271-00-2 (PB)

ISBN 978-1-964271-01-9 (eB)

All Scriptures given are from The King James Version of the Bible.

I would like to dedicate this book to the readers. I would also like to dedicate it to My Precious Mother and all of my family. And with all due gratitude, I would like to dedicate it to every person that is involved in the ministries worldwide. For their hard work, dedication, and love and kindness to all of those who sought the LORD, and found HIM as a result of the many great ministries out there.

May GOD Bless You all beyond measure.

Sincerely In Christ,

Evangelist

Thomas Couch

REVIVE - ALL MINISTRIES

ISAIAH 57:15

Contents

Introduction

First and foremost, I am sharing this book, *Characteristics of Faith* with you because I feel that the Holy Spirit moved on me to write this book. I also believe that HE confirmed it by giving me divine revelation concerning the Scriptures that I used in this book. Not to mention that HE helped me organize it and finish it. And HE has also provided the people that will publish it and put it into your hands.

The overall purpose of *Characteristics of Faith* is to give you some insight as to what faith is, and to introduce you to Characteristics of Faith, and to show you how to increase your faith.

It is my prayer that *Characteristics of Faith* will bless you. But even if you only get one tiny little nugget out of it that you can apply to your Christian walk, then I will be satisfied that GOD used me as the vessel to give it to you.

Enjoy! And may GOD Bless You beyond measure.

Author/Evangelist

Thomas Couch

Chapter One

The Muscles of Faith

*H*EBREWS 11:1
Now faith is the Substance of things hoped for, the evidence of things not seen.

This verse in HEBREWS gives us one description of faith. It says faith is the "substance" of things "hoped" for, the "evidence" of things not seen. We can identify, by looking at this verse, that faith is a unit, one body with certain characteristics.

An example of this would be, you for instance, you are a human being, one unit, with certain characteristics. You have a body, a Spirit, a soul, you have eyes, a nose, arms, legs, ears, feet, and so forth.

All of these characteristics make up you as a whole. You could have elements of your characteristics that you may never even know about. You would have to get inside of your body to learn about them. It is the same with faith.

This verse in HEBREWS shows us faith (the body) and three characteristics of that body. We see the "substance of faith," "the hope of faith," and the "evidence of faith." We can only see three in this verse, but there are more "inside" the body that we will look at later.

"The Substance of Faith."

The word substance can be defined as a support, groundwork, a foundation, a basic quality, or part of something.

So then, Jesus must be the substance of our faith. MATTHEW 7:24-27 says:

v. 24, Therefore whosoever heareth these sayings of mine, and doeth them, I will liken him unto a wise man, which built his house upon a rock:

v. 25, And the rain descended, and the floods came, and the winds blew, and beat upon that house; and it fell not: for it was founded upon a rock.

v. 26, And everyone that heareth these sayings of mine, and doeth them not, shall be likened unto a foolish man, which built his house upon the sand:

v. 27, And the rain descended, and the floods came, and the winds blew, and beat upon that house; and it fell: and great was the fall of it.

Look at verse 24, the house that was built upon the rock, the solid foundation. Jesus is that foundation - Rock.

Look at the rock mentioned in the book of EXODUS, it is an example, a type of Christ, EXODUS 17:6:

v. 6 Behold, I will stand before thee there upon the rock in Horeb; and thou shalt smite the rock, and there shall come water out of it, that the people may drink. And Moses did so in the sight of Israel.

With that in mind, look at ISAIAH 53:4. It says:

v. 4, Surely he hath borne our griefs, and carried our sorrows: yet we did esteem him stricken, smitten of God, and afflicted.

Now, with those two thoughts in mind, look at JOHN 4:14. It says:

v. 14, But whosoever drinketh of the water that I shall give him shall never thirst; but the water that I shall give him shall be in him a well of water springing up into everlasting life.

So here we see a rock smitten and water flowing out of it and we see Jesus smitten and water flowing out of HIM. The Rock, The Solid Foundation, The "substance of your faith," Jesus!

You must have that "substance" - foundation, The Rock, Jesus, for your faith to be whole. Look at MATTHEW 7:25, it says:

v. 25, And the rain descended, and the floods came, and the winds blew, and beat upon that house and it fell not: for it was founded upon a rock.

The house spoken of it this verse can be replaced with the word (Faith). The rain will come, the floods will come and the winds will blow and beat upon your faith. So if you do not want your faith to fall, you must have this important Characteristic, (The Substance). Your faith must be built on the Solid Rock. Jesus has to be the substance and foundation of your faith.

The following verses show us what will happen to our faith if we do not build on the substance (foundation), Jesus.

MATTHEW 14:26-27 says:

v. 26, And everyone that heareth these sayings of mine, and doeth them not, shall be likened unto a foolish man, which built his house upon the sand:

v. 27 And the rain descended, and the floods came, and the winds blew, and beat upon that house; and it fell: and great was the fall of it.

So if you have not built your house, your faith, on Jesus, when the rain comes and the floods come and when the winds blow and beats on your faith, it will fall. You can count on it.

Jesus is the substance of your faith, and your faith must be built on HIM. That means you must know HIM as your Lord and Savior. You must know HIM as your King of kings and Lord of lords. You must have a personal relationship with HIM. You must trust HIM and HIS Holy Word. And everything you do must be in HIS name.

Some of you may think you know HIM, you may think you have your faith built on a rock. But, you may be sitting on sinking sand and the first strong wind or hard rain may blow you down.

If you just see Jesus as a man who died on a cross a long time ago, then you are on the sinking sand. If you just see Jesus as a popular character in the Bible, you are on the sinking sand.

Before you go any further, I ask you to examine yourself and your faith. Please examine your relationship with Jesus. Do you have a personal, intimate relationship with HIM? Do you walk with HIM? Do You talk with HIM? Do you hear HIM when HE speaks to you? Do you really have the "substance" of your faith active in your life?

You need to know and be one hundred percent certain that you have Jesus, the substance of your faith active in your life.

When HE is active in your life, then you will be able to speak to your mountains and tell them to be moved out of your life, "In The Name Of Jesus," and they will have to move. When you have Jesus - the "substance of faith," active in your life, then you can ask GOD for anything, "In The Name Of Jesus" and HE will do it. But, always remember, the Power that makes things happen is "Jesus' name." So never, ever get the big head and think that you yourself do miracles. Everything has to be done In The Name of Jesus, and Jesus, not you, must get the glory for it.

Now, let's look at HEBREWS 12:2. It says:

v. 2, Looking unto Jesus, the author and finisher of our faith; who for the joy that was set before Him endured the Cross, despising the shame, and is set down at the right hand of the throne of God.

So, what we have covered this far gives new meaning to this verse. Jesus - (The Substance), is the author and finisher of our faith. The substance is what makes our faith grow. If you don't have this characteristic active in your faith, then your faith has not even begun to grow and it will not even begin to grow. Jesus is the substance and the author and finisher of your faith.

Jesus is the muscles of our faith. Our muscles are a tissue in our body, (faith) that we flex to move our body, (faith) to exercise a force. If you do not have muscles, there is many things you will not be able to do.

Let's look at PHILIPPIANS 4:13. It says:

v. 13, I can do all things "through" Christ which strengtheneth me.

The focus here is not on what we can do ourselves, as much as it is on whether or not we are doing it "through" Jesus and HIS strength. Jesus has all the Power, and we can do all things "through" HIS Power, it is HIS Power (muscles) that strengthens us.

HE is the muscles of our faith that cause the Spiritual force of faith to move mountains and manifest healing and blessings in our lives.

Some people may have the "substance", the muscles, "Jesus", in their lives and not even be flexing them.

You have got to flex the name of "Jesus" to exert the force of your faith. You can pray for three days, kick your feet, beat on the wall, everything, but, if you do not end it by saying, "In Jesus' Name" I Pray and flex your muscles it will all be in vain.

Flex Your Muscles!

Chapter Two

The Hands of Faith

H EBREWS 11:1
    Now faith is the "substance" of things "hoped" for, the evidence of things not seen.

Brace yourself now, because it may take you a moment to get this. But, according to this verse, just as Jesus is the substance of your faith, - "your faith is the substance of your hope." That is what it says, it says, "Now faith is the substance of things hoped for."

"The hope of faith."

There are two kinds of hope. One is the kind where the individual yearns or longs for something. You will have to have this kind to obtain the other kind. The other kind of hope I am talking about is the kind where the individual knows and has confidence and assurance that their faith is going to get them what they need. This hope is indeed a characteristic of your faith.

Let's look at MARK 11:22-24. It says:

v. 22, And Jesus answering saith unto them, Have "Faith" in God.

v. 23, For verily I say unto you, That whosoever shall say unto this mountain, Be thou removed, and be thou cast into the sea; and shall not doubt in his heart, but shall believe that those things which he saith shall come to pass, he shall have whatsoever he saith.

v. 24, Therefore I say unto you, what things soever ye desire, when ye pray believe that ye receive them, and you shall have them.

Now, I told you that there were three characteristics of your faith seen in HEBREWS 11:1. The first one was the substance, we have already covered that. So then the second characteristic we see in that verse is the Hope: of your faith.

Look at verse 22 that you just read from MARK. Jesus gives you the substance of your hope.

HE said to have "faith" in GOD. Faith is the substance of things "hoped" for. Jesus is telling you, "Have some," get it, obtain it and use your muscles." You can use them to do things like HE is showing them in verse 23.

v. 23, For verily I say unto you, that whosoever shall say unto this mountain, Be thou removed, and be thou cast into the sea; and shall not doubt in his heart, but shall believe that those things which he saith shall come to pass, he shall have whatsoever he saith.

First in verse 22, Jesus gave them faith, then in v. 23, HE shows them how it works. If you look closely, you will see both kinds of hope, the second characteristic of your faith active in this passage.

I told you there were two kinds of hope and you must have one to get the other. The first kind moves, then the second kind moves, then whatever you are standing in faith for manifests.

Look closely at v. 23, The first kind of "hope" moves, the yearning, the longing to have the mountain moved. Then the second kind of "hope" is activated and you believe it, you have confidence and assurance that your faith is going to function properly and manifest your need. Once those two characteristics of your faith are activated and you do not doubt it, Jesus said that you "shall," not might, but "shall" have whatsoever you saith, it "will" come to pass.

And if that was not enough, Jesus goes the extra mile and repeats it. HE shows us again in v. 24 "both" kinds of hope. The second characteristic of our faith in operation to receive whatever we are standing in faith for. It says:

v. 24, Therefore I say unto you, what things soever ye "desire", when ye pray, "believe" that ye receive them, and ye shall have them.

Look closely, the first kind of hope is activated, you "desire" it, you yearn for it, you long for it, that is the first kind of hope. Then you see the second kind of hope activated, you "believe" it, you have confidence, you are assured that you have it. Then you see what happens, it says, "and ye "shall" have them."

Ye "shall" receive them! If you receive something, you have it in your hands. "Your hope is the 'hands' of your faith."

First, you use your muscles, the name of Jesus. Then, your muscles flex and move your hope (hands) to receive whatever you are standing in faith for. And you get it!

Open Your Hands!

Chapter Three

The Heart of Faith

*H*EBREWS 11:1
      Now faith is the "substance" of things "hoped" for, the evidence of things not seen.

The third characteristic of your faith that we see in HEBREWS 11:1 is "Evidence." The evidence of things not seen.

Once you learn about these characteristics of your faith, then apply them and have them active in your life, you will "know" that you can have whatever need you are standing in faith for.

The word of GOD is the third characteristic of your faith (The Evidence). Let's look at what Jesus said about this evidence. MATTHEW 24:35, it says:

v. 35, Heaven and earth shall pass away, but my words shall not pass away. "GOD'S Word."

Jesus said the evidence (Word of GOD) of your faith is here to stay. It was here before you knew it was. And it will be here when the rain comes, it will be here when the floods come, and it will be here when the winds blow against your faith.

And not only will it be here when you are gone, but according to this verse in MATTHEW, it will be here when this heaven and earth are gone. That is what it says, "Heaven and earth shall pass away, but my words shall not pass away."

Look at what the Lord said in ISAIAH about HIS words. ISAIAH 55:10-11, it says:

v. 10, For as the rain cometh down, and the snow from heaven, and returneth not thither, but watereth the earth and maketh it bring forth and bud, that it may give seed to the sower, and bread to the eater:

v. 11, So shall my word be that goeth forth out of my mouth: it shall not return unto me void, but it shall accomplish that which I please, and it shall prosper in the thing whereto I sent it.

Verse 10 says, for as the rain cometh down, from heaven, (The evidence), the Word of GOD has come down from heaven and it is here to stay. The evidence (word) is powerful, and it is compared to rain in these verses.

Do you remember what happened to the faith mentioned earlier when the rain came, the word came and it was not founded on a solid foundation? The rain (Word of GOD) came and beat against that faith and it fell. The evidence (Word of GOD), the third characteristic of your faith, is powerful. It is the evidence of the things you cannot see, the things you hope for, "In the Name of Jesus."

The Word of GOD is the evidence, proof, of whatever you are standing in faith for. This verse in ISAIAH says:

v. 11, So shall my word, evidence, proof, be that goeth forth out of my mouth: it "shall" not return unto me void, but it "shall" accomplish that which I please, and it "shall" prosper in the "thing" whereto I sent it.

The evidence is already here. The end of this verse says it "shall" prosper in the "thing" whereto I "<u>sent</u>" it. Past tense, HE has already sent it. This verse says it shall prosper "<u>in</u>" the "<u>thing</u>" whereto I sent it. The thing it is "<u>in</u>" is your faith, the evidence of your faith, Word of GOD, the third Characteristic of your faith shall prosper. You may need to read that again to grasp the reality of it. The Word of GOD is, the evidence, the proof that you can have whatever you pray for or speak to and command to come to or leave your life.

Now we southerners call it a "thang," the thing, "Word of GOD "in" your faith, that third Characteristic, in your faith is that thang. Have you ever heard southerners proclaim victory from a ball game or something? Man they will get all excited and say, "boy oh boy, we put that thang on them." Glory to GOD! When you have that "thang" active in your faith, that third Characteristic, the evidence, the Word of GOD, active in your faith, then you can speak to that mountain and put that "thang" on that situation. That "thang" shall accomplish whatever GOD pleases it to accomplish and that "thang" the Word of GOD "shall" prosper "<u>in</u>" your faith. Glory to GOD!

The Word of GOD, the evidence, the third characteristic of your faith is the heart of your faith.

Let me say it again: "The Word of GOD is the heart of your faith."

A heart is an organ with "muscles". Ring a bell? A heart has muscles because it is always working, it never stops beating till your flesh dies. Imagine what the muscles in your arms would look like if they were constantly working out with weights. Even while you slept, your arms were continuously working out with weights. Awesome thought, huh?

Well, that is the way your fleshly heart is, and it is the same way with the heart of your faith. The muscle of your faith, heart, "Jesus" is continuously flexing to keep "the blood" of Jesus flowing into whatever you are standing in faith for. Glory to GOD!

Let's look at REVELATION 12:11, it says:

v. 11, And they overcame him by the blood of the Lamb, and by the word of their testimony; and they loved not their lives unto the death.

When your faith is whole, the heart is pumping; the muscles are flexing and the hope is alive and active. You can have the victory over the devil. This verse says, "and they overcame him, 'the devil', by the blood of the Lamb, AND by the word of their testimony." The word of your testimony is "the Word of GOD in your life." And what the Word of GOD has done for you. The Word of GOD active in your life, the heart, will pump the blood of Jesus into "anything" the devil may bring at you, and you will overcome Him by the blood of The Lamb and the word of your testimony, which is The Word of GOD active in your faith.

Let's look at PROVERBS 4:23, it says:

v. 23, Keep thy heart with all diligence; for out of it are the issues of life.

Now look at PROVERBS 3:3, it says:

v. 3, Let not mercy and truth forsake thee; bind them about thy neck; write them upon the table of thine heart.

So, you get the Word of GOD, mercy and truth in your heart according to verse 3:3 that you justread. Then verse 4:23 says out of the heart "are" the issues of life. Another way to put it would be, out of the heart "are" the issues of "faith". Your faith! It does not say out of it "will be", in the future, or that it will be coming in the future. It says out of the heart "are", present tense, here and now, are the issues of your faith. It is the evidence of things not seen. The Word of GOD. The heart of your faith. Glory to GOD!

Open Your Heart!

Chapter Four

The Revelation of Faith

R EVELATION 1:19
Write the things which thou hast seen, and the things which are, and the things which shall be hereafter;

When the Lord spoke to me and said, "I want you to write a book on faith," I was quick to say, "O.K. Lord, I will."

So, I started looking up what I could find from the dictionary and other things. But what I found really wasn't enough. I found the Greek word for faith and two or three definitions and stuff like that, but it was not enough. So, I said, "Lord, this is not much to write about. How can I write a book on faith on such a small amount of information on the subject?" So HE said to me, "I will show you!" So as I laid on my bed, I asked The Lord to show me what Faith is. This is what the Spirit of GOD gave me.

Faith is the -

- Fearless

- Anointed

- Identifying

- Their

- Hope

The Lord gave me five *Characteristics of Faith*. It actually took that divine revelation a few days to sink into my little finite mind. Then I analyzed those characteristics for a few days. Then I finally sat down to write this book, "Characteristics of Faith."

I prayed about it and, being a little familiar with HEBREWS Chapter Eleven, I turned to it, looked at verse one and The Holy Spirit gave me three more characteristics of faith, which I have already given you in the first three chapters.

The next five chapters will be on these five characteristics that I have just given you, and I pray that you will enjoy these characteristics and divine revelations just as much as I am enjoying receiving them and giving them to you. Glory to GOD!

I asked The Lord about faith and I said, "Lord, how big is faith?" HE said to me, "it is so big, that just a small amount the size of a mustard seed can move mountains. My dear Christian friend, mountains are "big". You have little hills and slopes and so forth, but a mountain can be "miles" high and round, that is big!

So if just a tiny amount of Faith can move huge mountains, just imagine, "if you can," what miles high and round amounts of faith could accomplish. I will tell you what it could accomplish, miracles, miracles, and miracles is what a large amount of faith will accomplish.

Look at Jesus, HE had a large amount of faith. That is how HE done the miracles HE did. We can have a large amount of faith, too.

Let's look at MATTHEW 14:15-16, it says:

v. 15, And when it was evening, his disciples came to him, saying, this is a desert place, and the time is now past; Send the multitude away, that they may go into the villages, and buy themselves victuals.

v. 16, But Jesus said unto them, They need not depart; give ye them to eat.

Jesus said, "Give ye," you give them to eat. But, the disciples did not have all the Characteristics of big faith active in their faith. So they did not know what to do. They could have done the miracle themselves or Jesus would not have told them, "Give ye," you give them to eat. Jesus knew that they did not have enough food to feed them. There were five thousand men, not counting women and children, there. Jesus and the disciples were traveling on foot, and there was no way they could have carried enough food to feed all of those people. But Jesus knew that they were capable of doing the same miracle that HE was going to do. That is why HE told them, "give ye," you give them to eat.

But, when Jesus saw that their faith was not whole, HE told them to give HIM what little food they had and HE took it, blessed it, showed them what big faith could do and gave it back to them, and they fed five thousand men, not counting women and children. That is the kind of big miracles that big faith can manifest. Those disciples could have done it, and you and I should be able to do it today.

Did you know that most of the miracles the people in the Bible received was manifested according to "their" faith?

Let's look at MATTHEW 9:20-22, it says:

v. 20, And, behold a woman, which was diseased with an issue of blood twelve years, came behind him, and touched the hem of his garment:

v. 21, For she said within herself, If I may but touch his garment, I shall be whole.

v. 22, But Jesus turned him about and when He saw her, he said, Daughter, be of good comfort; "thy faith" hath made thee whole. And the woman was made whole from that hour.

My dear Christian friend, I have just showed you that "you" can have big miracle working faith for yourself. This woman had that disease for twelve years before she finally got a hold of it and had all the Characteristics of her faith active in her life. Then her faith became big enough to manifest her miracle of healing.

My prayer is that this book, "Characteristics of Faith," will help you to enlarge your amount of faith to an amount big enough that you can overcome a disease or problem before it even has a chance to impose a threat to you. Or if you already have a problem, it will help you get the victory over that problem manifested in your life. So you won't have to struggle with it for twelve years or longer like this woman did. It took her twelve years to increase the amount of faith she had, to an amount of faith that she needed to be healed.

So I encourage you to enlarge your faith, you my dear Christian friend, "you" can have big faith too.

Imagine this if you can. The earth is the size of a mustard seed compared to the size of faith.

Praise The Lord!

Faith Is Big!

Chapter Five

The Fearlessness
of Faith

1 st JOHN 4:18

There is no fear in love; but perfect love casteth out fear: because fear hath torment. He that feareth is not made perfect in love.

Fearlessness is the fourth characteristic of faith that I will show you. Whole faith is fearless! Another way to look at this verse would be like this:

"There is no fear in "faith", but perfect "faith" casteth out fear: because fear hath torment. He that feareth is not made perfect in "faith."

Let's look for a minute at what fear does to faith. Look at MATTHEW 14:22-30, it says:

v. 22, And straightway Jesus constrained his disciples to get into a ship, and to go before him unto the other side, while he sent the multitude away.

v. 23, And when he had sent the multitudes away, he went up into a mountain apart to pray: and when the evening was come, he was there alone.

v. 24, But the ship was now in the midst of the sea, tossed with waves: for the wind was contrary.

v. 25, And in the fourth watch of the night Jesus went unto them, walking on the sea.

v. 26, And when the disciples saw him walking on the sea, they were troubled, saying, it is a Spirit; and they cried out for fear.

v. 27, But straightway Jesus spake unto them, saying, Be of good cheer; it is I; be not afraid.

v. 28, And Peter answered him and said, Lord, if it be thou, bid me come unto thee on the water.

v. 29, And he said, come. And when Peter was come down out of the ship, he walked on the water to go to Jesus.

v. 30, But when he saw the wind boisterous, he was afraid; and beginning to sink, he cried, saying, Lord, save me.

This, my dear friend, is what fear will do to your faith. Look at verse twenty-seven, when Jesus approached them, they cried out for "fear", and Jesus spoke to them and said, "be not afraid." So Peter answered HIM and asked if it was HIM to bid him to step out in faith and walk on the water to where Jesus was (verse twenty-eight). Then Jesus told him to come in verse twenty-nine, and Peter stepped out in faith and was walking on the water. But look at verse 30, Peter let fear cause his faith to fail. It says, "he was afraid"; and beginning to sink. Peter became afraid, and that fear caused his faith to fail him right in the middle of a faith miracle. If he had not have let fear in, he could have run all over the place "on the water," jumped for joy, turned flips and just had a blast in that faith miracle. But fear made his faith fail, and it robbed him of his blessing.

Now, let's look at a very popular verse in the book of JAMES to support what I am showing you. Look at JAMES 2:20, it says:

v. 20, But wilt thou know, O vain man, that faith without works is dead.

Another way to look at this would be to say; "faith without love is fearful, "dead". You may say to me, you are just bending the Scriptures all out of whack; no I am not. I am showing you a mystery of the Kingdom that the Holy Spirit has revealed to me. You see, if perfect love casteth out fear, and fear is what will cause your faith to fail and be dead, then you must have that perfect love that only the Holy Spirit can give, in order to have fearless faith, "Big" faith.

If you will look, in the book of JOHN, you will see that Peter did not yet have perfect love, and that was what caused his faith to fail him my dear friend.

Let's look at JOHN 21:15-17, it says:

v. 15, So when they had dined, Jesus saith to Simon Peter, Simon, son of Jonas, lovest thou me more than these? He saith unto him, yea, Lord; thou knowest that I love thee. He saith unto him, feed my lambs.

v. 16, He saith to him again the second time, Simon, son of Jonas, lovest thou me? He saith unto him, yea, Lord; thou knowest that I love thee. He saith unto him, Feed my sheep.

v. 17, He saith unto him the third time. Simon, son of Jonas, lovest thou me? Peter was grieved because he said unto him the third time, Lovest thou me? And he said unto him, Lord, thou knowest all things: thou knowest that I love thee. Jesus saith unto him, feed my sheep.

O.K., do you remember what happened in MATTHEW? First, Jesus told the disciples to feed his sheep, (the people), but the disciples did not have "big" faith, so they did not know how to feed all those people like Jesus had told them to do. Although, they could have done that same miracle. Then when they left that place where Jesus showed them what "big" faith could do, is when Jesus went to them on the water, the same passage, and Peter's fear, "lack of love" caused him to lose his faith miracle on the water.

So, here in this passage, Jesus shows him the ingredient he needed to do the same miracles HE had done, "feed the sheep." HE asked Peter three times if he loved HIM. Then when Peter realized that Jesus was actually showing him his weakness, that he was "lacking in love", he went on the defense and said, "Lord you know all things, you know that I love thee."

But, Jesus did not pat him on the back and say, Oh I know you love me. Jesus responded with another command, "Feed my Sheep." Jesus "knew" that Peter was not walking in love yet. HE saw the fear in Peter's life and the fear was evidence that Peter was not walking in love and the fear was evidence that his faith was not big. His faith kept failing him time and time again. Fear was what even caused Peter to deny Jesus, Praise GOD! Jesus "knew" that Peter was full of fear, that is why Jesus could Prophesy and tell Peter before it ever happened, you "will" deny me three times.

Have you ever asked someone something and you know that when they answered, they were not telling the truth? You may ask them a second time, are you sure?, or even a third time are you sure?

You may even say, now, now, are you sure about that?, just to try to get the truth out of them. It is kind of like catching a child with his hand in the cookie jar, standing there with chocolate all over his mouth and hands, and you ask them what they are doing. They will be fast to say "nothing", but you know differently, the fact is obvious. Well, that is what Jesus was doing with Peter in this passage. When we get close to Jesus, "The True Light, " all of our spots and blemishes start showing.

Jesus was saying, "do you love me?" Peter says yes! Jesus says, "your fears say differently." Then Jesus would give him the command, "feed my sheep." Do the miracles that I do! Show me love in your faith! Love not fear!

A lot of people will tell you that Peter was restored in this passage, but that was not the case. Peter's weakness was exposed in this passage, that he was not yet walking in love because of his fear.

Peter gave a common human response. Look at what Peter did. Look at JOHN 21:21-22:

v. 21, Peter seeing him saith to Jesus, Lord, and what shall this man do?

v. 22, Jesus saith unto him, If I will that he tarry till I come, what is that to thee? "Follow thou me."

Peter was convicted and he asked Jesus, "what about this man," (take the focus off of me), this man has weaknesses too, what about him, what shall he do? Jesus told him "don't" worry about him yet, you are not made perfect in love yet, you cannot feed the sheep yet, you're not really concerned about him, you follow me! So, Jesus exposed him again. See, Peter was not asking Jesus about that other disciple because he was concerned about him, Peter was trying to shift the focus off of himself. But, Jesus "knew" it and Jesus gave Peter the solution, "follow thou me."

Keep following me! You will eventually receive the Holy Spirit and start walking in love, and your faith will get big, and you will be able to "feed my sheep" and do the same miracles that I do.

Jesus said it himself. Look at JOHN 14:12, it says:

v. 12, Verily, verily, I say unto you, He that believeth on me, the works that I do shall he do also; and greater works than these shall he do; because I go unto my Father.

Then in JOHN 14:15, Jesus said if you love me, keep my Commandments. I showed you one commandment that HE gave us, as HE gave it to Peter. "Feed my Sheep," do the same miracles that I do!

Praise GOD! If you want to see when Peter was really restored and started walking in love and fearless faith, just read ACTS Chapters One and Two. It was when Peter received The Holy Spirit that he was restored, and he started "feeding the sheep," doing miracles. That was when Peter was restored.

Love and fearlessness is the fourth Characteristic of Faith.

Love and do not fear, and your faith will grow, grow, grow.

Faith Is Fearless!

Chapter Six

The Anointing of Faith

2 *nd CORINTHIANS 1:21*
    Now he which stablisheth us with you in Christ, and hath anointed us, is God.

Being anointed is the fifth characteristic of faith. The anointing is a very, very important characteristic of your faith. You really need to acknowledge this and have the anointing of Jesus active in your life in order to have whole faith.

Let's look at this verse in 2nd CORINTHIANS 1:21. It says:

v. 21, Now he which stablisheth us with you in Christ, an hath anointed us, is God.

According to this Scripture, "GOD" does the anointing for faith. "GOD", The Holy Spirit, is the one who anointed Jesus. That is why you do not read anywhere in the Gospels where a man anointed HIM, like they did the earlier Prophets. That is why Jesus' anointing for faith was complete and HE could manifest the miracles that HE did.

Let's read on down and I will show you why the Holy Spirit must give you the anointing for faith. In the same passage, 2nd CORINTHIANS 1:21-24, it says:

v. 21, Now he which stablisheth us with you in Christ, and hath anointed us, is God;

v. 22, who hath also sealed us, and given the earnest of the Spirit in our hearts.

v. 23, Moreover I call God for a record upon my soul. That to spare you I came not as yet unto Corinth.

v. 24, Not for that we have dominion over your "faith", but are helpers of your joy: for by "faith" ye stand.

This passage is clearly about the faith anointing. According to this passage, "GOD" has put a special anointing in your faith, to stablish you in Christ." The Holy Spirit in our hearts provides a special faith anointing to each individual in Christ. Verse Twenty four says, "Not for that we have dominion over your "faith". So you see, no one else can exercise your faith. No one else has dominion over it to do the things GOD wants to do through you. Not only that, but the last half of that, verse twenty-four, says: "for by 'faith' ye stand."

So, my dear Christian friend, you will need this special faith anointing to stand. It is given to help us stand in every area of our lives.

Let's look at some of the things the Word of GOD says we are going to need a special faith anointing to stand against.

Look at EPHESIANS 6:10-17, it says:

v. 10, Finally, my brethren be strong in The Lord, and in the power of his might.

v. 11, Put on the whole armour of God, that ye may be able to "stand" against the "wiles of the devil."

v. 12, For we wrestle not against flesh and blood, but against "Principalities," against "Powers," against the "rulers of the darkness" of this world, against "Spiritual wickedness" in high places.

v. 13, Wherefore take unto you the whole armour of God, that ye may be able to "withstand" in the evil day, and having done all, to "stand".

v. 14, "Stand" therefore, having your loins girt about with truth, and having on the breastplate of righteousness;

v. 15, And your feet shod with the preparation of the gospel of peace;

v. 16, "Above all", taking the shield of faith, wherewith ye shall be able to quench "all" the fiery darts of the wicked.

v. 17, And take the helmet of Salvation, and the sword of the Spirit, which is the word of God.

Do you recall what I said earlier in chapter four? I said that my Prayer is that this book *Characteristics of Faith* will help you to enlarge your amount of faith to an amount big enough that you can overcome a disease or problem before it even has a chance to impose a threat to you. Or if you already have a problem, it will help you get the victory over that problem manifested in your life. So you won't have to struggle with it for twelve years or longer like the woman with the issue of blood did.

That is what the anointing of faith does. Read this passage again. EPHESIANS 6:10-17, verse eleven says, that we will be "standing" against the wiles of the devil. That includes sickness, poverty attacks, attempts to destroy relationships, attempts to rob you of your faith, miracles and blessings, and above all, to get you to doubt what GOD said to you and attempts to turn you away from GOD. Those are just a few of the wiles of the devil. You must have the faith anointing to "stand" against all those evil Spiritual forces that mete out those kinds of things in a Christian's life.

What I really want you to focus on now is verse 16. EPHESIANS 6:16, it says:

v. 16, "Above all," taking the shield of "faith," wherewith ye shall be able to quench "all" the fiery darts of the wicked.

Another way to look at this would be to read it like this, "Above all," taking the "anointing of faith", wherewith ye shall be able to quench "all" the fiery darts of the wicked.

This verse says, "Above all, you must have the 'shield' (anointing) of faith, then you will be able to 'quench all' the fiery darts of the wicked."

When you get this special faith anointing, you will be able to "quench", (Put out) "all", not some, but "all" the evil things the devil will try to bring into your life. When you get this special faith anointing, you will be able to crush adversity before it even gets started.

Jesus "knew" that HE was anointed. Jesus also knew, that The Spirit of GOD had anointed HIM and what GOD had anointed HIM to do. It was Prophesied in the book of ISAIAH that GOD would anoint HIM to do specific things. (ISAIAH 61:1-2). Then, in the Gospel of LUKE, Jesus proclaimed it and then fulfilled it. Let's look at LUKE 4:18-21, it says:

v. 18, The Spirit of the Lord is upon me, because "he" hath "anointed" me to Preach the gospel to the poor; he hath sent me to heal the brokenhearted, to preach deliverance to the captives, and recovering of sight to the blind, to set at liberty them that are bruised.

v. 19, To preach the acceptable year of the Lord.

v. 20, And he closed the book, and he gave it again to the minister, and sat down. And the eyes of all them that were in the synagogue were fastened on him.

v. 21, And he began to say unto them, This day is this scripture fulfilled in your ears.

Jesus applied the Word of GOD to HIS life right here in this passage. And what I want you to focus on is in verses 18 and 21. In verse 18, Jesus said The Spirit of The Lord is upon me, because "he" hath anointed me. Stop right there. HE has anointed me. Then look at verse 21, Jesus says, And he began to say unto them, This day is this scripture "fulfilled" in your hearing. Glory to GOD!

When Jesus applied the Word of GOD to HIS life, it was fulfilled that same day.

Now, my dear Christian friend, let's look at that verse again in 2nd CORINTHIANS 1:21. It says:

v. 21, Now he which stablisheth us with you in Christ, and "hath anointed us", is God.

Glory to GOD! People, you can stand up and quote this verse and apply it to your life, just like Jesus did. You can say, the Spirit of the Lord is upon me, because "he has anointed" "me" to do everything the Word of GOD says I can do. Praise GOD All Mighty! When you do this, it "will" be fulfilled in your life.

You may say, but not me. I just don't think I can do any miracles. My friend, that is not what the Word of GOD says.

Let's look at MARK 16:15-18, it says:

v. 15, And he "Jesus" said unto them, Go ye into all the world, and preach the gospel to every creature. Jesus,

v. 16, He that believeth and is baptized shall be saved; but he that believeth not shall be damned.

v. 17, And these signs shall follow them that believe; In my name shall they cast out devils; they shall speak with new tongues;

v. 18, They shall take up serpents; and if they drink any deadly thing, it shall not hurt them; they shall lay hands on the sick, and they shall recover.

Now don't you get too high-minded. Jesus said in verse 17, In HIS name. HE said it is in HIS name, "The name of Jesus," that we will do those things. But in the same respect, you are the one who will have to do it.

It is kind of like this: if you have a car, you will also have keys for it. But if you do not apply that key to the ignition, then you are not going anywhere. You can get behind the wheel and make noises that sound like the motor. You can lean forward and scoot up and try to scoot it along, but you won't ever move that car. But Praise GOD, when you apply that key and start the car, then you can "travel". You can take the combination of the key and the car and do things.

Some people have the name of Jesus and do not even apply it. They are just sitting behind the wheel making noises. But let me tell you my dear Christian friend, you can take the faith anointing, (the car), and the name of Jesus, (the key), and you can combine them and apply them and Praise GOD "you" my dear Christian friend can do miracles. The Bible, The Word of GOD, said it, not me! So Praise GOD you can believe it! 2nd CORINTHIANS 1:21 says GOD will anoint you with that powerful faith anointing to do everything HIS word says you can do. Praise GOD!

Faith Is Anointed!

Chapter Seven

The Identification
of Faith

R *OMANS 12:3*

For I say through the grace given unto me, to every man that is among you, not to think of himself more highly than he ought to think; but to think soberly, according as God hath dealt to every man the measure of faith.

Identification of faith is the sixth characteristic of faith that I will give to you. What I am saying to you is that faith is identifiable. According to this verse in ROMANS, GOD has dealt to every man the measure of faith. It is kind of like the car and the key example I gave you. You are a Christian and you have been given faith, but if you have not identified it yet, then you cannot use it yet.

Jesus identified the amount of faith that the people had. Look at MATTHEW 6:30, it says:

v. 30, Wherefore, if God so clothe the grass of the field, which today, is, and tomorrow is cast into the oven, shall he not much more clothe you, "O ye of little faith"?

This is one example of Jesus identifying their faith and HE said to them, "O ye of little faith". Let's look at another example where Jesus identified someone's faith. Look at MATTHEW 8:26, it says:

v. 26, And he saith unto them "why are ye fearful, O ye of little faith"?

So Praise GOD, not only could Jesus identify their faith, HE could identify which characteristics of faith it was that they lacked. Here in this verse, Jesus asked them why were they so fearful. So Bless GOD, HE knew by the presence of fear that they were lacking in love, and look at what HE said to them, "O ye of little faith".

Let's look at another example of Jesus identifying the people's faith. Look at MATTHEW 14:31, it says:

v. 31, And immediately Jesus stretched forth his hand, and caught him, and said unto him "O thou of little faith", wherefore didst thou doubt.

So here we see when Jesus identified Peter's faith, Jesus saw the fear and the doubt, and he knew that Peter's faith was little faith. Jesus knew that the presence of fear showed the lack of love and Jesus knew that the doubt was from them not having and trusting in the evidence of their faith. So Praise GOD, here again we see Jesus identifying someone's faith and the lack of the Characteristics needed to have whole faith. And look at what he said again, "O ye of little faith".

Let's look at another example of Jesus identifying someone's faith. Look at MATTHEW 16:8, it says:

v. 8, Which when Jesus perceived, he said unto them, "O ye of little faith", why reason ye among yourselves, because ye have brought no bread?

Here again, Jesus identifies their faith. It says, "when Jesus perceived", you could look at it this way also, and say, "when Jesus identified", He said unto them "O ye of little faith". Jesus identified the lack of the evidence of faith, "The Word of GOD", and trusting in it was present. Because they could not understand or discern what HE was saying to them. HE was talking to them about doctrine, which if they had have known the "evidence", Word of GOD, they would have known that the doctrine of the Pharisees and of the Sadducees were not in line with the Word of GOD. Jesus could see the lack of that characteristic of faith. If HE had not, then HE would not have had to warn them. And look again at what Jesus said to them, "O ye of little faith".

The flip side of this is, every time Jesus said to them "O ye of little faith," HE was saying, why is your faith so small or little? Praise GOD, you can have bigger faith. You can have stronger faith. Praise GOD.

So you see by these verses that faith is identifiable. So just like Jesus saw the people's faith, you and I can see each others faith. However, we do not need to focus on someone else's faith. We need to be learning all we can and identifying our own faith.

Let's see what the Bible says about us looking at our own faith. Look at a verse in 2nd CORINTHIANS 13:5, it says:

v. 5, Examine "yourselves", whether ye be in the "faith"; Prove your own selves. Know ye not your own selves, how that Jesus Christ is in you, except ye be reprobates.

According to this verse, we are to examine our own faith, prove our own selves. Paul even uses a little sarcasm in this verse. He says; "Know ye not your own selves". He is saying, Know ye not your own faith! Examine yourself. Do you have whole faith? Do you have the Characteristics of Faith alive and active in your life? If not, then according to the last part of this verse, you may be in a reprobate state of faith. That means that you are out of reach of the voice of GOD, you won't do what the Bible says to do, you may be living an immoral lifestyle and do not realize you need to change. But you can examine your faith and these characteristics that I am giving you could be a good starting place. Being in a reprobate state of faith is a bad place to be in, because, like I said, you cannot hear the voice of GOD. So then it may be the voice of disaster that GOD needs to allow you to hear to draw you back into the faith.

My dear Christian friend, you have already seen that you can identify your faith and the Characteristics of your faith. Now allow me to show you that once you identify your own faith, and the Characteristics of your Faith, then you can be assured that you have the faith you need to do whatever GOD'S Word says you can do. Look again at ROMANS 12:3, it says:

v. 3, For I say through the grace given unto me, to every man that is among you, not to think of himself more highly than he ought to think; but to think soberly, according as God hath dealt to every man the measure of faith.

So you see here that GOD has given everyone the measure of faith. HE has already given it to you. But you have to apply HIS word and activate those characteristics of faith in your life. And each time you do, your faith will grow. The Apostles asked Jesus one time to increase their faith. But HE did not do it for them. What Jesus did was, HE told them what their small amount of faith could do.

Let's look at it in LUKE 17:5-6;

v. 5, And the apostles said unto the Lord, increase our faith.

v. 6, And the Lord said, If ye had faith as a grain of mustard seed, ye might say unto this sycamine tree, Be thou plucked up by the root, and be thou planted in the sea; and it should obey you.

They had asked Jesus to increase their faith. But Jesus didn't, HE simply told them in a roundabout way, you do it! By giving them an example of what their faith could do. Jesus was saying try it, exercise it yourself, and examine it. Then the last part of the verse says and "it should obey you". Whatever you speak to in faith should obey you, if you just have a tiny bit of faith. They asked Jesus to increase their faith, but Jesus put it right back on them. "You do it," HE said. Examine your own faith and when you find out what is lacking, get that characteristic and exercise it in your faith and increase your own faith.

If you want to do everything you can to increase your faith, the first thing you need to do is read the Word of GOD, the Bible, "regularly". Look at ROMANS 10:17, it says:

v. 17, So then faith cometh by hearing, and hearing by the word of God.

So the first step to increasing your faith is getting in the Word of GOD. Then you need to start exercising your faith. You will have to say, Praise GOD I am going to exercise my faith in this situation, I don't care who sees me or what they think and even if it doesn't happen right now, then I am still going to believe that it will happen, eventually. And you start speaking to situations and exercising your faith and eventually you will start seeing it work and your faith will start increasing and you will start stepping out and speaking to bigger things and those things will start obeying you and Praise GOD before you know it, your faith will have increased and it will continue to increase for the rest of your life on earth.

I told you earlier that you could be assured that you have faith. I say to you now that you can be "fully" assured that you have faith. I have already showed you that GOD has dealt to everyone the measure of faith. So let's look at a verse now that says you can be fully assured of your faith. Look at HEBREWS 10:22, it says:

v. 22, Let us draw near with a true heart in "full assurance of faith", having our hearts sprinkled from an evil conscience, and our bodies washed with pure water.

What I want you to focus on, is those words, "Full assurance of Faith". So you see, you can be "fully" assured that you have faith. Oh, you have it and you can identify it and you can increase it. You can identify the characteristics of faith and you can examine it for yourself. Praise GOD! Identify your Faith.

"Faith Is Identifiable"

Chapter Eight

The Personalization of Faith

R OMANS 12:3

For I say through the grace given unto me, to every man that is among you not to think of himself more highly than he ought to think; but to think soberly, according as God hath dealt to every man the measure of faith.

According to this verse, GOD has dealt to "every" man, Christian, the measure of faith. It is yours and it is up to you to keep it functioning in your life.

First, you have to receive this, you have to realize that you already have faith. GOD gave it to you! Stop talking about it like it is something you might obtain in the future. Make it personal! Personalize your faith! It is yours personally and no one else's.

Look at it this way. Let's use the car example again. GOD has given you a car; you are going to have to use the keys; you are going to have to put the gas in it, you are going to have to put oil in it, and new tires on it, and you are going to have to operate it. You are going to have to push the gas pedal and the brakes, and change the gears, and "you" have to make sure it is equipped to run. Then you have to operate it. It is "your" car. No one else is going to put gas and oil and tires and things on it for you so you can drive it. You have to do it! Then when you get behind the wheel, no one is going to reach down there and push the gas and brakes for you. You must do it yourself. It is the same with faith.

GOD has given you, *every* man, *every* woman, *every* Christian, the measure of faith. It is "yours" personally. You have the responsibility of getting to know your faith and what makes it work. The characteristics of faith are what make it work. And the lack of those characteristics is what will make faith fail. Let's look at an example of someone's personal faith failing them. Look at the passage in LUKE 22:31-34, it says:

v. 31, And the Lord said, Simon, Simon, behold, Satan hath desired to have you, that he may sift you as wheat:

v. 32, But I have prayed for thee, that "thy" faith fail not: and when thou art converted, strengthen thy brethren.

v. 33, And he said unto him, Lord, I am ready to go with thee, both into prison, and to death.

v. 34, And he said, I tell thee, Peter, the cock shall not crow this day, before that thou shalt thrice deny that thou knowest me.

Look closely at this passage, verse 32: Jesus said "thy" faith fails not. You see, it was not that Peter was going to lose his faith and then find it later. Jesus prayed that Peter would learn how to operate "his" faith so he would not keep failing at everything. Then in the second half of that same verse, verse 32, Jesus told Peter, and when thou art converted, strengthen thy brethren.

Peter had already been converted. But Jesus had prayed for his faith to become big and HE knew that eventually Peter's faith would be bigger (converted) from failing faith, to victorious, conquering faith. That was a faith confession that Jesus made right there in verse 32. First, HE prayed for Peter, then HE told Peter "when it happens", you help other people. Jesus "knew" it would eventually happen. And Peter was restored and his faith was converted (strengthened) over in the book of ACTS.

Peter finally got a hold of the fact that faith was "his" personal gift from GOD. And Praise GOD let's look at what he did when he learned how to operate it. He did just exactly what Jesus told him to do. He strengthened the brethren. Look at what Peter wrote in his book. Look at 2nd PETER 1:5-7, it says:

v. 5, And besides this, giving all diligence, "add to your faith" virtue; and to virtue knowledge;

v. 6, And to knowledge temperance; and to temperance patience; and to patience godliness;

v. 7, And to godliness brotherly kindness; and to brotherly kindness Charity.

Praise GOD! Peter finally got a hold of it. That it was "his" faith, and he started telling people how they could have big faith. He said in verse 5, add to "your" faith. Praise GOD, add this characteristic, add that characteristic, here is another characteristic. Add it, add, add, add and Praise GOD keep on adding, and your faith will increase.

Glory to GOD! Peter personalized his faith, then he found out that it had a few characteristics. Then he applied those things to his faith, and miracles started happening. Then here in his book, Peter done exactly what Jesus told him to do. Peter started giving you and I those characteristics of faith to add to our own personal faith, which is exactly what the purpose of this book is. It is to give you "Characteristics of Faith" to add to your own personal faith, so you can do and receive all that GOD'S word says you can do and have. And so that you can quench "all" the evil darts that Satan will throw at you while you are here on this earth. When you see those evil darts of debt, sickness, trouble, whatever, coming your way, then you can speak the Word of GOD to them in faith and watch them fall to the ground, they will get behind you and be only a part of your past. You will be able to quench them, put them out, before they have any effect on your life.

Glory to GOD! I am talking about the seventh Characteristic of Faith. Make it personal!

"Big Faith is Personalized!"

Chapter Nine

The Hope of Faith

*C*OLOSSIANS 1:23

If ye continue in the "faith" grounded and settled, and be not moved away from the "hope of the gospel", which ye have heard, and which was preached to every creature which is under heaven; whereof I Paul am made a minister;

According to this verse, the hope of the gospel is another characteristic of faith. It says "if you continue in the faith grounded and settled"; if you are grounded and settled, you won't be moved away from the hope of the gospel. But, if you are not grounded and settled and you are moved away from the hope of the gospel, then you may not continue in faith.

Your faith may become stagnant, it won't change or grow. It is evident that we need these characteristics of faith active in our faith to be able to do the things GOD'S Word says we can do.

Well you may say, what is the hope of the gospel that we need to be able to continue in faith? The hope of the gospel is, "The hope of Eternal Life". Look at what Paul said in ACTS 23:6, it says

v. 6, But when Paul perceived that the one part were sadducees and the other Pharisees, he cried out in the Council, Men and brethren, I am a Pharisee, the son of a Pharisee: of the hope and resurrection of the dead I am called in question.

See, Paul; made a confession here in this verse. That his faith was built around Jesus and HIS bodily resurrection. The hope of the gospel, which is a characteristic of faith that we need to continue in faith. Paul was saying that he had this hope, the hope of Eternal Life, and that was what he was being called into question about.

Let's look again at what Paul said about his hope of Eternal Life. Look at ROMANS 8:21-25, it says:

v. 21, Because the creature itself also shall be delivered from the bondage of corruption into the glorious liberty of the children of God.

v. 22, For we know that the whole creation groaneth and travaileth in pain together until now.

v. 23, And not only they, but ourselves also, which have the first fruits of the Spirit, even we ourselves groan within ourselves, waiting for the adoption, to wit, the redemption of our body.

v. 24, For we are saved by hope: but hope that is seen is not hope: for what a man seeth, why doth he yet hope for?

v. 25, But if we hope for that we see not, then do we with patience wait for it.

You see, Paul is confessing here that he has that hope of the gospel, the hope of Eternal Life. You must have this Characteristic of Faith active in your faith to continue to grow. The hope of the gospel, the hope of Eternal Life.

Let's look again at what Paul said about this Characteristic in TITUS 1:1-2, it says:

v. 1, Paul, a servant of God, and an apostle of Jesus Christ, "according to the faith of God's elect", and the acknowledging of the truth which is after godliness;

v. 2, "In hope of eternal life", which God, that cannot lie, promised before the world began;

Paul was confessing to have this characteristic of faith active in his faith. What he was saying was, GOD promised it and he, himself, knew without a doubt that he had it active in his faith.

Look at how he started this epistle. He said, "according to the "faith" of God's elect", and the acknowledging of the truth which is after godliness.

Paul was saying, according to the "faith" of GOD'S elect, I have become who I am in Christ, a servant of GOD and an apostle of Jesus Christ and I am acknowledging the truth which is after godliness, another way to put it would be, I am acknowledging the truth which is after "god-likeness". Having the Characteristics of GOD.

But verse 2 tells how he is doing it, according to faith. Verse 2 says, "In hope of Eternal Life", In this Characteristic of Faith, the Characteristic that GOD promised us before the world began, "and that I now have". Paul had it and he "knew" without a doubt that he had it.

This Characteristic of Faith is the hope of the gospel, which is the hope of Eternal Life, and you can know without a doubt that you have it. Let's look at what the Word of GOD says about it in another book. Look at 1st JOHN 5:13, it says:

v. 13, These things I have written unto you that believe on the name of the son of God; that ye may "know" that ye have eternal life, and that ye may believe on the name of the Son of God.

For us believers, we can know without a doubt that we have Eternal Life. And this Characteristic of Faith that we will need to continue in faith. We need it to grow in faith. We need it, to have big faith.

"Big Faith Has Hope!"

Chapter Ten

Add, Add, Add!

2nd PETER 1:5

And besides this, giving all diligence, "add" to your faith virtue; and to virtue knowledge.

My Dear Christian Friend, I have to confess to you that, even though the Lord has used me as the vessel to point out these Characteristics of Faith to you. Personally, my faith is still growing. I am still having to add a little love here and a little forgiveness there and a little kindness over there.

One thing we need to remember is that we are never to look down on anyone with little faith. We are to have compassion on them and encourage them in the Word. Do not ever look down on anyone for being sick or uneducated or in debt or anything like that. Look at what ROMANS 12:3 says about it:

v. 3, For I say through the grace given unto me, to every man that is among you, "not to think of himself more highly" than he ought to think; but to think soberly, according as God hath dealt to every man the measure of faith.

Do not ever think too highly of yourself because of the great faith you may have. Do not ever think that you are better than anybody else!

To be totally honest with you, I personally believe this adding to our faith will be a life long thing for us. Because once we do achieve big miracle working faith, then each new miracle that we perform is a new Characteristic of Faith that we have just added to our own individual faith.

You see, we know that the gift of miracles is a Spiritual gift. Look at this verse in 1st CORINTHIANS 12:10, it says:

v. 10, To another the "working of miracles"; to another Prophecy; to another discerning of Spirits; to another divers kinds of tongues; to another interpretation of tongues:

So you see that working of miracles is a gift of the Spirit. O.K. Now let's look at why the gifts of the Spirit are given to us. Look at EPHESIANS 4:12, it says:

v. 12, For the perfecting of the Saints, for the work of the ministry, for the edifying of the body of Christ.

See, your faith is one of the main things that the gifts work to perfect. Once you start working small miracles, you start perfecting your faith. Each little miracle you work becomes a new Characteristic of Faith for you and it will help your faith grow.

Do you remember what I said earlier about there being elements of your Characteristics of Faith that you may never know about? Like I said, each new miracle you manifest by faith will be added to your faith. Those are Characteristics that will help you overcome doubt. Because you will see them manifest in the natural realm in your life. You will be able to identify doubt when it comes, and you will be able to say, "well Praise GOD it worked the first time and it will work again."

If you are standing in faith for something that has not come to pass yet, The Word of GOD states that you have got to keep believing you have it until it comes to pass. ROMANS Chapter 4 says, that GOD, Himself calls those things which be not as though they are. And you can look at it, the Bible says it, not me. ROMANS 4:17, it says:

v. 17, (As it is written, I have made thee a father of many nations), before him whom he believed, even God, who quickeneth the dead, and "calleth those things which be not as though they were."

So, if you have prayed for something and you are standing in faith for it, dear Christian you must keep calling it as if you already have it. Keep confessing it until it comes to pass. Look at what Jesus Himself said about it. Look at MARK 11:22-24, it says:

v. 22, And Jesus answering saith unto them, Have faith in God.

v. 23, For verily I say unto you, that whosoever shall say unto this mountain, Be thou removed, and be thou cast into the sea; and shall not doubt in his heart, but shall believe that those things which he saith shall come to pass, he shall have whatsoever he saith.

v. 24, Therefore I say unto you, what things so ever ye desire, when ye pray, believe that ye receive them, and ye shall have them.

Look at verse 23, it says that once you speak to it, and shall not doubt in your heart, but shall believe that those things which he saith shall come to pass. It says, "come to pass"! That means that if it does not happen right then, that it will in the future, "come to pass". And you shall have whatsoever you say!

It may be that you are lacking in one of the Characteristics of Faith that is causing the delay of your faith miracle. But, do not give up! Keep on believing it and keep on calling it as though you already have it!

It may not even be you that is causing the delay. The angels may be in battle trying to manifest your faith miracle. But keep on believing for it and do not doubt, keep on calling it as if you already have it!

I told you earlier that you can have big miracle working faith. But then I told you that I believed we will be adding to our faith all of our lives. That may sound like a contradiction, but it is not. Because you see, faith is so big that it only takes a small, tiny bit to move mountains. Jesus said that Himself. You may be one of those that Jesus refers to as a "ye of little faith", but keep in mind that a tiny little bit of faith the size of a mustard seed can still do miracles. You can too! Keep in mind also, that you do not have to accept little faith, you can add to it and it will grow.

Look at what Peter wrote in 2nd PETER 1:5-7, it says:

v. 5, And besides this, giving all diligence, "add" to your "faith" virtue; and to virtue knowledge;

v. 6, And to knowledge temperance; and to temperance patience; and to patience godliness;

v. 7, And to godliness brotherly kindness; and to brotherly kindness Charity.

My Dear Christian Friend, right here is "seven" more Characteristics of Faith that we are told to "add" to our faith. And Praise GOD the list goes on and on. The Word of GOD is just full of Characteristics of Faith that you and I will continue to add to our faith. Look at the Fruit of the Spirit in GALATIANS Chapter 5, more Characteristics of Faith for us to add to our faith. We have Love, Joy, Peace, Long-suffering, Gentleness, Goodness, Faith, Meekness and Temperance. Here we have nine (9) more Characteristics of Faith that we can add to our faith. I know what you are thinking right now, so let me explain. You are thinking, well how do you add faith to your faith? Well that goes back to adding each new miracle you experience as a new Characteristic of Faith. It is a "faith miracle". So you are adding a "faith" miracle to faith. So you see, you can add faith to faith.

There are more Characteristics of faith we can add to our faith. The gifts of the Spirit. The commands that GOD'S Word gives us to live by to perfect us. While we do them, it not only perfects us, but it perfects our faith. And it is indeed a life long experience. But during that life span, you may see many or few faith miracles of your own. That is between you and GOD!

Let me give you a perfect example of what I am talking about. Everybody knows who Moses is, and all the miracles that he did. Look in HEBREWS 11:24-29, it says:

v. 24, "By faith" Moses, when he was come to years, refused to be called the son of Pharaoh's daughter;

v. 25, Choosing rather to suffer affliction with the People of God, than to enjoy the pleasures of sin for a season;

v. 26, Esteeming the reproach of Christ greater riches than the treasures in Egypt: for he had respect unto the recompence of the reward.

v. 27, "By faith" he forsook Egypt, not fearing the wrath of the King: for he endured, as seeing him who is invisible.

v. 28, "Through faith" he kept the passover, and the sprinkling of blood, lest he that destroyed the firstborn should touch them.

v. 29, "By faith" they passed through the Red Sea as by dry land: which the Egyptians assaying to do were drowned.

So you see, Moses had faith. He saw miracle after miracle. All of those big miracles that Moses saw were done by faith. But, even after all that Moses had seen, look at what he said at the end of his life, in his old age. Look at DEUTERONOMY 3:24, it says:

v. 24, O Lord God, thou hast "begun" to shew thy servant thy greatness, and thy mighty hand: for what God is there in heaven or in earth, that can do according to thy works, and according to thy might?

Moses had seen miracle after miracle, he saw GOD move time and time again. But here in this verse, at the end of his life, in his old age, Moses said, "O Lord God, thou hast "begun" to shew thy servant thy greatness. How could Moses say that GOD had just "begun" to show him HIS greatness after all Moses had seen? It was because it is a life long thing! So you see, even in Moses' old age, he proclaimed that GOD had begun to show him HIS greatness.

You and I will be the same way my Dear Christian Friend. We will be adding to our faith all of our lives, and we will see GOD move time and time again.

You know, in my personal opinion, I believe GOD may have given Moses a glimpse of heaven, and that may have been what made Moses say that GOD had just begun to show him HIS greatness.

You see, in this passage, Moses was telling the people how he had prayed to GOD and asked GOD to allow him to go over the river into the Promise Land. That is in DEUTERONOMY Chapter 3. Look at what GOD told Moses, DEUTERONOMY 3:27, it says:

v. 27, Get thee up into the top of Pisgah, and lift "up" thine eyes westward, and northward, and southward, and eastward, and behold it with thine eyes: for thou shalt not go over this Jordan.

I think that GOD showed Moses a glimpse of heaven in this verse. HE told Moses to lift "up" his eyes, look up, and look in all directions and behold it with thine eyes. But thou shall not go over "this" Jordan. I believe that GOD may have been telling Moses, you will not go over "this" Jordan that you are asking to go over. But GOD was showing Moses the real Promise Land that he would be going to "in heaven".

I say this because we know from the Bible that Moses did not get to go to the Promise Land here on earth. But we also know that Moses is in Heaven. Look at MATTHEW 17:1-3, it says:

v. 1, And after six days Jesus taketh Peter, James, and John his brother, and bringeth them up into an high mountain apart.

v. 2, And was transfigured before them: and his face did shine as the sun, and his raiment was white as the light.

v. 3, And behold, there appeared unto them "Moses" and Elias talking with him.

So you see, Moses has to be in Heaven, if he wasn't, then he would be in hell and no one returns from there.

I told you these things because I personally believe that GOD showed Moses, at the end of his life, how he would go to Heaven instead of the earthly Promise Land. I believe GOD showed Moses that last and final faith miracle he was going to experience on earth. As he passed from Mortal to Immortality in Heaven, GOD showed him that final faith miracle that we all long to see. And Moses responded by saying "O Lord God", thou hast "begun" to shew thy servant thy greatness. Praise GOD!

Let's look at a verse that applies to you and I in this same respect. Look at EPHESIANS 2:8, it says:

v. 8, For by grace are ye saved "through faith"; and that not of yourselves; it is the gift of God:

This is a Scripture that says that we are promised to be saved. Through faith! This verse is ours right now, but it will be manifested at the end of our lives. Because, hell and eternal damnation is what we are saved from. Heaven is our place of deliverance from going to hell. We are not there yet, but we "know" we will be going there at the very end of our lives "through faith"! At the very end of our lives, you and I will see the ultimate faith miracle. Praise GOD! But for now, we have got to keep adding to our faith. Glory to GOD!

"Add, Add, Add!"

Power Prayer

For Salvation and to be baptized in the Holy Spirit.

Father GOD, I come to you as humbly as I know how. Lord, your word says in 1st JOHN 1:9, "If we confess our sins, he is faithful and just to forgive us our sins, and to cleanse us from all unrighteousness." So I confess to you that I have sinned in many ways. I now repent and turn away from my sins and I ask you to forgive me and cleanse me from all of my unrighteousness, in the name of Jesus?

Father, your word also says in ROMANS 10:9-10, "That if thou shalt confess with thy mouth the Lord Jesus, and shalt believe in thine heart that GOD raised HIM from the dead, thou shalt be saved. For with the heart man believeth unto righteousness; and with the mouth confession is made unto Salvation."

So I confess with my mouth that I believe Jesus died on the Cross so I can be saved and I believe with all my heart that GOD raised HIM from the dead and I ask you to come into my life and save me? I now accept Jesus as my Lord and Savior and I believe with all my heart that your word is true and that I am saved by grace!

Father, your word also says in the book of LUKE 11:13, "If ye then being evil, know how to give good gifts unto your children: how much more shall your heavenly Father give the Holy Spirit to them that ask him?"

So Father, I ask you to give me the gift of the Holy Spirit? I ask you to fill me till my cup runs over and allow me to successfully function in the gifts of the Spirit that are mentioned in your word? So that I will become an effective witness for Jesus and a blessing to others for the rest of my life? In Jesus' name I pray, Amen?

If you prayed this prayer, you can believe without a doubt that you are saved. The Bible says "you shall be saved". That is a promise and it is also a promise that GOD will fill you with the Holy Spirit if you ask HIM.

So now you need to join a good Church and sincerely turn away from your old sinful life and walk in and enjoy the new Spirit filled life that GOD has given you. The old you should start fading into the past, and the new you will start shining brightly as you seek to serve GOD in all you do.

About the author

Thomas Couch has attended Mercer University and Brewton Parker University. He currently runs a ministry called REVIVE-ALL Ministries, an outreach of "Souls Harbor Word of Faith Church" in Canton, Georgia, where he was ordained and licensed to minister as a Preacher of The Gospel. He holds a Certificate in Caring for People God's Way with Light University, which is approved by the American Association of Christian Counselors Board.

Couch is an active member of the Colorful Crow Writers Community and is engaged in a writing ministry. He has been blessed with the task of writing material as a ministry to God's people, to reach the lost, and to abundantly bless all who will enjoy his writing.

He says it is proof that with GOD you can do all things through Christ who strengthens you (Philippians 4:13) and he prays it will be a blessing to everyone whom it reaches.

www.ingramcontent.com/pod-product-compliance
Lightning Source LLC
Chambersburg PA
CBHW051333120626
46547CB00016B/2529